FUN FACTS AND USEFUL INFORMATION

Cool Stories and stuff you didn't know

****

TABLE OF CONTENTS

WHY READ THIS BOOK?

I put together this book because; most people want to learn about things we don't know. Even as a kid I loved to read about these things. The Book of world records has been one of my favorite reads. I will share with you many subjects to peak your interest in fun facts and useful information.

We will cover

- The Earth.
- Geography
- History
- Food
- People
- Animals
- Plants
- Science
- Space
- Technology
- The Universe
- Weather
- Sports
- And a misc category for other stuff.

You will be interested and you will learn as you read.

As you read through the book, you will learn about many things you didn't know. You can read it anytime you want to learn something cool. You will have a place to look when you want to learn something new.

Grab a copy of Fun facts and useful information now and learn about what you didn't know.

ANIMALS

The common frilled shark has the longest gestation time of any animal. They are pregnant for 42 months. The elephant is second with a 22 month gestation period.

The world's most dangerous animal. It is not what you would think. The mosquito is the most deadly. All the variety of mosquitos and the diseases they carry have killed up to 50% of all humans excluding wars and accidents since the stone age.

The Goliath bird eating tarantula can weigh up to 6 oz. and be the size of a large dinner plate. It feeds on birds in the coastal rainforests of Suriname, Guyana, French Guiana, Brazil and Venezuela.

A Goliath Bird eating tarantula

The wolf spider is a common poisonous spider found in America and Europe. The spider is poisonous, but a bite is not fatal. The wolf spider is different because it doesn't make a web. It is a hunter and will hunt its food instead of catch it.

An aardvark can eat over 100,000 ants and or termites in one meal. The also eat a fruit called the aardvark cucumber. The plant requires them to dig it up, eat it and then poop out the seeds to keep the cycle of the plant surviving. An aardvark is not the same as an anteater. They are unrelated.

Black widow spiders are very poisonous. They are also in many parts of the world. They will be in wood piles or wooden outhouse buildings. Thanks to indoor plumbing, black widow bites are very rare now.

Termite mounds in Australia can be up to 20 feet high and up to 100 feet around. The mounds are complex structures with gardens, basements, and nurseries. They have ventilation shafts brooding chambers and a royal palace where the queen termite lives. The mounds are made of saliva and clay.

Gorillas are the largest animal to build a nest. They build a new nest every evening. Gorillas build ground nests, they don't sleep in the trees. They build it out of plant material close to where they are feeding. Adult gorillas sleep in their own nest. Babies sleep with their mother until they are 3.

Male monarch butterflies migrate from Mexico all the way to central Ontario Canada. This migration covers 3,000 miles or more. They winter in Mexico and migrate all over the United States and Canada in the spring and summer.

The arctic tern migrates from the arctic circle to Antarctica and back each year. This migration covers 50,000 to 70,000 miles per year.

Humpback whales migrate from warm water breeding grounds to the colder northern feeding grounds every year. Swimming up to 6,000 miles back and forth.

The Tardigrade is the hardiest animal there is. They have been in space on the outside of the rocket ship. They survived in the vacuum of space and enough solar radiation to kill anything accept them. Of the ones sent on the trip, more than a third of them survived the trip.

African wild dogs are the most effective hunters of all large predators. They live in packs of 20 to 40 dogs and succeed in 80% of their hunts. It's disturbing to watch them hunt and eat. They don't kill the prey first. The attack and tear off pieces of flesh while the prey is still alive and keep doing it until the prey dies. They are also great at stealing other animals meals. They are not hyenas.

Nine banded armadillos always have quadruplets, and they are always all the same sex. They dig burros and stay underground during the day and come out at dusk to forage for food. They eat bugs and carry leprosy.

A badger can do something special. If they are being attacked by a larger predator, they can dig their way into the ground backwards and forward. So they can dig into the ground while fighting off the attacker. They will eat just about anything they can kill, but a big part of their diet are earthworms.

Bats are the only mammal that can fly. There are over 1000 species of bats, and they live in almost every part of the world. Small bats are insect eaters. Large bats are fruit eaters. Most people are squeamish about bats, but it is possible that without the millions of bats in the world eating mosquitoes, the humans may not survive all the disease that mosquitoes would spread.

Black bears have a sense of smell 7 times better than a bloodhound. They can smell humans and other bears up to 5 miles away when the wind is right. Most black bears are black, but the farther west in the United States you go the bears are more brown. Their color can be close to grizzly bears, but not as big. Black bears eat berries, roots and fruit, and meat.

The African buffalo, or cape buffalo is the most dangerous animal to people in Africa. The cape buffalo kills more hunters than any of the other big game animals in Africa. It is a relative of the American buffalo and are both related to the cow. The cape buffalo is the only African cow like an animal. Cape buffalos are social and friendly and will protect others of their group. They are not social with people.

There are two types of old world camels. The dromedary and the Bactrian camels. The best way to remember which has one hump and which has two is by using the capitalized letter of their name flipped 90 degrees counterclockwise. D and B. If you lay the D on its back it has one hump, dromedary. If you lay the B on its back, there are 2 humps.

Cheetah is the fastest animal on earth. They can go from standing still to 60 mph in 3 seconds. They can run up to 70 mph for a couple hundred yards before they overheat and need to stop. Many times they have their kill stolen while they are resting after a kill and a hard run. Male cheetahs are social and will live in groups. Females are not social most of the time, except for a short time when breading. The Cheetah has claws that do not retract like other cats; they are always out.

One of the determining factors to determine if a cat if a large cat or a small cat is if they can roar. A cougar or mountain lion is bigger than a leopard, but the cougar can't roar and the leopard can. The leopard is a large cat the cougar is not. They can growl and make other noises, but if you have ever heard a lion or a tiger roar, it is very different.

There are 40 different species of Dolphins. The largest is the killer whale. They are smart. They will hunt in packs, and can force schools of fish into shallow water where they are food for the dolphins. Bottlenose dolphins are the most well know. Dolphins are popular because of the tv show flipper, and can learn to do many things.

The largest of all land animals is the African elephant. They weigh in at around 200 pounds at birth. They will gain up to 2 pounds per day. The African elephant will continue to grow and gain mass into their 30s. They can top out in the 12,000 pound weight area when full grown.

The giraffe has the highest blood pressure of any animal. The average blood pressure of a giraffe is 240/180. Their heart has to pump their blood up to 7 feet from the heart to the brain. To do this, they have a large powerful heart, up to two feet long. They have a special valve in their neck that closes when they bend over to regulate the blood pumping to their brain.

Gorillas are the largest of the great apes. They can weigh up to 600 pounds. Gorillas are herbivores, although from checking feces, they eat small creatures. They will eat up to 50 pounds of vegetation per day. Gorillas will only sleep in a nest one night. Only females with young will share. All other make and sleep in their own nest every day.

Grizzly bears are very large bears. They are not as big as the Kodiak bears. Both are part of the group of brown bears. The grizzly has a hump in the upper part of the back where their front leg muscles attach. These large muscles give them the strongest from legs of any animal. They get less active in the winter, but they do not hibernate.

A full grown hippo is 14 to 16 feet long and will weigh about 4,000 pounds. Hippos will spend up to 16 hours a day in the water, but they don't swim. They push off the bottom and drift, or walk along the bottom of the river. They have a sensitive outer layer of skin that requires them to have a water source to keep the skin wet. Hippos are the most dangerous animal in Africa as far as killing people. They kill 2,900 people per year, not to eat, they only eat plants. They are mean and nasty.

The polar bear is the largest of all the bears. Polar bears eat almost only meat, seals to be exact. And not even any seals, they eat ringed seals and bearded seals. The seals live under the ice and the polar bears feed on the ice of the arctic. Polar bears can smell a seal from half a mile away. When the ice melts, the polar bears eat little until the ice returns.

Rhinos are the second largest land animal. There are 5 species of rhinos, the two most common are the white and black. Both are gray. The black ones are muddy most of the time, it makes them look black. They are not aggressive with humans, but they are not friendly, and should have plenty of room if you encounter them. Rhinos have an area they mark as their own that covers about 5 square miles.

 The walrus is a social animal. They spend one third of their lives sleeping almost on top of each other. They can dive to a depth of over 300 feet to get small creatures off the bottom.

In studies of ostriches, they studied 200,000 ostriches over 80 years and never seen a single one bury their head in the sand.

Rats multiply fast. Over a period of a year and a half, two rats can have over a million descendants.

A duck's quack does not have an echo, and scientists can't figure out why.

Crocodiles can't move their tongue, and can't chew. They tear off pieces of flesh and bone and their stomach juices will digest just about anything.

A group of 12 or more cows is a flink. There only needs to be 2 cows to call them a herd.

Donkeys are such good animals on mountain trails because of where their eyes are. They can see all four of their feet at the same time.

A strong male lion can mate 50 times a day. That's why the females do all the hunting.

Polar bear fur looks white, but is colorless, the hollow tubes of fur scatter light making it appear white.

A polar bear can run at speeds up to 25 mph, and swim at speeds up to 6 mph.

A polar bear has an acute sense of smell. They can smell a seal up to a mile away. They can even smell them under water.

Polar bears spend most their lives alone. Other than when they are ready to mate.

Polar bears are the most carnivorous bears. The eat leaves and seaweed and berries in the summer, they prefer to eat seals. They are the least efficient hunters. Only about 2% of their hunts succeed. They can go months without eating if they need to.

Snakes are true carnivores. They eat no plant material, only meat.

A eagle can kill a small deer and fly carrying it. I was fishing this past summer, and an eagle flew past in front of me carrying a muskrat or a beaver. It was at least 5 pounds.

When hippos get angry, their sweat turns red.

EARTH

The world's highest mountain varies depending on how you measure it. Everest is the highest from sea level. It is not the highest if you go from the center of the earth.

Mt. Chimborazo in Ecuador is higher than Everest. Because of a bubble in the earth's crust it is higher than Everest.

The tallest mountain on earth is Mauna Kea, a volcano in Hawaii, if measured from the base of the mountain. It is almost a mile taller than Everest if measured from the base at the bottom of the ocean.

The largest desert on earth. A desert is an area that has no or little rainfall. By definition, Antarctica is the largest desert on earth at 5.4 million square miles. The largest hot desert is the Sahara at 3.5 million square miles.

The Pacific is the largest ocean on earth. It covers an area of over 160 million square miles. It is also the deepest on average, with an average depth of over 13,000 feet.

The deepest spot is also in the Pacific ocean. It is the marianas trench. Located off the coast of Japan, it is over 36,000 feet deep. The pressure at the bottom of the trench is around 1,000 time what it is on the surface.

What color is water? Many things can change the color of water, but water is blue. Not because of reflecting the color of the sky, but because water absorbs the red light, so we see the opposite color, blue.

The Pacific ring of fire is a concentrated ring of volcanoes and earth activity. It stretches for over 24,000 miles and contains 452 volcanoes. Over 75% of the active volcanoes in the world are in this ring.

Japan has 10% of the world's active volcanoes, and experiences over 1,500 earthquakes per year. Because of the earthquakes and volcanoes, they also experience tsunamis that can devastate.

Australia is the least volcanic active place on earth. They have had no eruptions for over 5,000 years.

Australia is also the flattest continental land mass. The average elevation is 652 feet above sea level, with the highest point on the continent Mt. Kosciuszko at 7,300 feet above sea level.

The Dzungarian basin in the Uygur region of China is 1,645 miles from the nearest open sea. It is the farthest place on earth from open sea.

The longest mountain range on the earth's surface is the Andes mountains. They stretch for 4,700 miles and go through 7 countries. They have an average height of 13,000 feet, with over 50 peaks over 20,000 feet high.

The world's most active volcano is Kilauea in Hawaii. It has been erupting since 1983.

The longest erupting volcano is Mt. Stromboli off the coast of Italy that has had mild emissions of gas and lava for close to 3,000 years.

Angel falls in Venezuela is the highest waterfall in the world. It has a total drop of 3,212 feet, with the highest single drop of over 2,600 feet. That is more than ½ a mile drop.

Angel falls

⅔ **of the geysers** in the world are in Yellowstone National Park in Wyoming.

The Nile is the longest river in the world. It starts at lake Victoria and flows 4,160 miles.

The Amazon is by far the largest river in the world. There are places where the Amazon is over 7 miles wide. The water flow of the Amazon is 60 times greater than the flow of the Nile.

The longest mountain range on Earth is the Mid Atlantic ridge. It is almost 25,000 miles long. Iceland

in the northern end of the range is the only part of it
that is above water.

FOOD

Graham crackers had a very interesting start. Graham was a minister who though because they were so bland, he could use them to help teenagers abstain from sex. It was to be birth control. The recipe has changed; they taste much different now than in the 1800s.

The average person will eat 2,200 chickens in your lifetime. Also on average one sheep, six ducks, nine cows and 63 turkeys.

Pound cake got its name from the ingredients. A pound of butter, a pound of flour, a pound of eggs, and a pound of sugar.

An ear of corn has an even number of rows, 16.

Titanium dioxide is in products to make them whiter. Things like sunscreen, paint, and ranch dressing.

In the 1800s, catsup was medicine. You can spell it ketchup or Catsup.

Carnauba wax used in car wax, shoe wax, and in fruit snacks.

Nutmeg in small doses causes no problems. Raw nutmeg in large doses can cause anxiety, confusion, headaches, nausea, dizziness, amnesia and hallucinogenic effects. The effects can take several hours to reach full effect and can last for several days. Careful.

Apples float because ¼ of the apples volume is air.

The 57 in Heinz 57 represents the number of the variety of pickles they once made.

Worcestershire sauce made by layering anchovies in brine with tamarinds fruit, molasses, garlic, vinegar, chilies, cloves, shallots and sugar. Its left sitting for 2 years with occasional stirring. It's not made like this anymore.

McDonald **sells** 75 hamburgers every second of every day.

Shellac is used to make the surface of jelly beans shiny.

Capsaicin found in peppers binds to the VR1 receptors in the skin. These are the nerve endings that tell us something is hot so we don't burn our skin.

Why do we like to eat spicy foods that make our brain think we are being burned? Studies have shown that it is masochism. That is why people try to go the highest level of pain they can endure.

Fortune cookies you get in Chinese restaurants are not from China. They first showed up in San Francisco in the early 1900s.

German chocolate cake has nothing to do with Germany. Samuel German is the creator of that type of cake.

Salted butter can be unrefrigerated for up to 2 weeks without fear of bacteria. Unsalted butter should stay in the refrigerator.

Bell pepper are not all the same. Some have three lobes and some have four. The 4 lobe ones are sweeter and better to eat raw. The three lobed ones are better cooked or grilled, and they have fewer seeds.

Almost everyone has gone to a Chinese restaurant and had General Tso's chicken. Unless you live in China. This is an American dish and is not at all Chinese. It is popular in America.

The average American drinks 58 gallons of water per year, and 44 gallons of soda per year. Up to 2013 it was about the opposite for the previous 2 decades.

GEOGRAPHY

Mount Thor in Canada on Baffin Island has the highest sheer vertical drop. 4,101 foot sheer cliff.

The dead sea is around 1400 feet below sea level and is getting lower by close to 3 ft per year.

Reno Nevada is 83 miles west of Los Angeles California. Look at a map.

More than half of all the freshwater lakes in the world are in Canada.

The Antarctic ice sheet covers about 5.5 million square miles. That ice sheet contains close to 90% of all the freshwater on Earth.

The full ceremonial name for the city of Bangkok in Thailand is *Krungthepmahanakhon Amonrattanakosin Mahintharayutthaya Mahadilokphop Noppharatratchathaniburirom Udomratchaniwetmahasathan Amonphimanawatansathit Sakkathattiyawitsanukamprasit.* It's a good thing they don't have to use that in an address on an envelope.

The shortest city name is Å. The town is both in Sweden and Norway.

There are 43 building in Manhattan that are so big they have their own zip code.

The Sargasso sea is in the North Atlantic ocean. The borders of the sea are 4 currents. It is the only sea that has no coast.

Istanbul Turkey is the only city in two continents. Part in Europe and part in Asia. The business part is in Europe and most of the people live on the Asian side.

 The United States and Canada share the world's longest border. 5,525 miles.

The highest recorded temp. On earth for many years was in Libya at 136 degrees. The record was not verifiable. The verified record occurred in death valley California at 134 degrees.

The lowest recorded temperature on earth was in Vostok Antarctica at -134 degrees. Interesting in that both are 134 degrees above and below zero.

The highest average temperature is in Western Australia where it is 96 degrees year round.

The Atacama desert in Chile is the driest place on earth. Parts of this desert have had no measurable rain since the late 1500s. The air is so dry the temperature varies from a high to a low of 50 degrees or more per day.

More than half of the coastline of the United States is in Alaska.

The Amazon river has so much water flowing into the ocean that up to 100 miles out to sea, you can still get fresh water.

The Amazon rainforest produces twenty percent of the earth's oxygen.

The country of Brazil got its name from the nut, not the other way around.

On the interstate highway system in the U.S. one mile every five miles has to be strait so it can be an emergency landing strips if needed in war or other emergencies.

In 1853 Captain Richard King purchased a ranch in southern Texas, 825,000 acres. It is the largest ranch in the U.S. 1,289 sq. miles.

The largest ranch in the world is in Australia. It covers six million acres. That area is larger than the country of Israel.

 Lake Baikal in Russia is the largest lake by water volume in the world. 20% of the non frozen fresh water in the world is in this lake. It has more water than all the great lakes in the United States combined..

At the closest point, the distance between Russia and The U. S is 2.4 miles. The 2 islands in the middle of the shot are the closest points of the 2 countries. The bigger island on the left is Russia, the smaller island is the United States. Big Diomede and Little Diomede Islands.

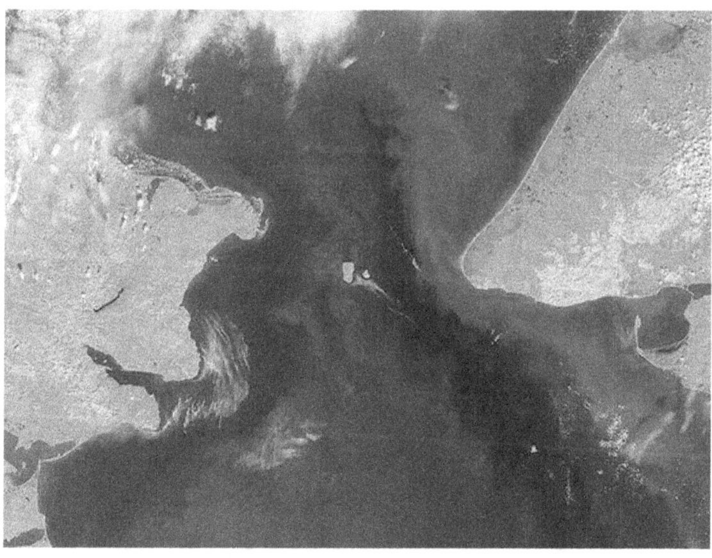

Satellite photo credit Nasa/ Wikimedia Commons

The pacific ocean is so massive, there is a few places you you went down and through the center of the earth and came through the other side, you would still be in the pacific ocean.

There is a fence in Australia that is 3,500 miles long. It is to protect sheep from the dingo.

The Grand Tsingy, or forest of knives is a razor sharp 325 square miles of limestone created by weathering over the years. The name Tsingy means where no one can walk.

HISTORY

The number of interesting things in this category are almost unlimited. There are so many things and many of them are unknown to most people. Here are some I think are the most interesting.

President Lincoln and President Kennedy similarities

You may have heard of this but the facts are amazing.

- The two presidents were second children in their families.
- They both served as boat captains.
- Both elected in the year 60. Lincoln in 1860, Kennedy in 1960
- Each had three children living with them in the white house. One child passed away while they were in office.
- Lincoln had a secretary named Kennedy. Kennedy had a secretary named Lincoln.
- Both assassinated in office.
- After their death, both succeeded by a man named Johnson.
- Both Andrew and Lyndon Johnson born in 08. Andrew Johnson in 1808, Lyndon Johnson in 1908.
- Both of their killers born in 39. John Wilkes Booth born in 1839. Lee Harvey Oswald born in 1939.
- Booth and Oswald assassinated before their trials.
- Both elected to congress in 46. Lincoln 1846, Kennedy 1946

- Both shot in the head, on Friday

These things are just a coincidence. But it makes for interesting facts.

When the post office started They had a weight limit of 50 pounds. They had to change rules after because people were sending children through the mail. It was a good way to send your kid to visit grandma. For 15 cents you could send them through the mail. The postmaster had to ban sending humans through the mail.

Mail order brides, were like modern dating websites. Men were moving west and needed wives and companions. There were few women in the west where the men were. The men would send letters to churches and groups back east to find single women. They would write back and forth for a while and if it seemed good, the women would travel west to be with the men. As the practice moved forward, there were women overseas that got involved. There were actual catalogs of women for the men to pick from.

MISC

The band Metallica has been a popular band for over 30 years. They have played sold out shows worldwide. They have done something that no other band has done. Played a show on all 7 continents. In 2013 the went to Antarctica and played a show for 120 scientists in a special dome. To not damage the environment, the show went on with no amplification. The audience had to listen through headphones. I am sure it took a lot from the Metallica experience. I have seen them live, and they put on a great show.

It was the second rock concert ever on the continent. The first concert in Antarctica was a group of scientists who formed a band.

American coins are unusual in that there is no numeric value on the coins as to their value. This causes problems with non-English reading people and people who can't read. The value is written but not in a numeric value. Most other coins from around the world have the value in numeric values. The size is also no sign. The dime is the smallest coin, but not the smallest value.

The American dime was first created from the first American coin, the silver dollar. The dime was 10% of the value, so the amount of silver was 10% of the silver used in a dollar. The other coins were created after to make transactions easier, but making a penny 1% of a dollar would have made the penny so small it would weigh.25 grams or.0088 oz. You would not hardly see them.

There has been talk about changing the coinage of the United States. The problems with the above issues, plus the cost of creating the coins is more than they are worth. It costs 9 cents to make a nickel and 1.66 cents to make a penny. It costs 5.66 cents to make a dime, and it costs only about 8 cents to make a quarter.

The most watched tv series shows in history were the final episode of MASH with over 50 million views, followed by the final episode of Cheer with over 40 million viewers.

Aardvark is the first word in the English dictionary.

 The fastest cycling across America by Rob Kish in 1992 in the race across America cycle race. He made the 2,911 mile trip in 8 days 3 hours and 11 min. He rode around 22 hour per day. He covered an amazing 360 miles per day.

Most people can't lick their elbow. Some say you can't do it, some have proven that a few people can. Over 75% or people who read this will try to lick their elbow.

27% of all food produced in western nations end up in the garbage.

Chihuahua desert in northern Mexico called the zone of silence. Radio signals don't come in this area. It is the site of several official meteorite impacts on earth. There are also several claims of actual alien encounters.

The first company created by Bill Gates called Traff-o-data. They produced the boxes that count traffic going by a spot on highways.

A ball of glass will bounce higher than a ball of rubber. A ball of steel will bounce higher than the rubber or the glass.

The name Wendy invented for the play Peter Pan in 1904. There is no recorded person with the name Wendy before that.

There are no English words in the dictionary that rhyme with orange, purple or silver.

Leonardo Di Vinci invented scissors.

Celery and apples burn more calories to eat than what the food contains.

Chewing gum while peeling onions will keep you from crying.

The Guinness book of records holds the record of being the most stolen book from public libraries.

The word queue is the only word in the English language that reads the same if you remove the last 2 or the last 4 letters of the word.

The word set has the most definitions of any word in the English language. Over 30.

Almost is the longest word in the English language with all the letters in alphabetical order.

Rhythm is the longest word in the English language without a vowel.

In 1386 a pig was executed in France by public hanging for the murder of a child.

You can't kill yourself by holding your breath. You will pass out and breathe again when you pass out if you can even hold it that long.

More people are allergic to cow's milk than any other food.

The strongest muscle in the human body is the tongue.

Humans and dolphins are the only species that have sex for pleasure.

Flying is the safest form of transportation. If you were to fly every day, the odds of being in a plane crash would take 100,000 years.

I am is the shortest complete sentence in the English language.

There is enough fuel in a full jumbo jet fuel tank to drive the average car 100,000 miles.

A rainbow is only visible in the morning or afternoon. The sun has to be at less than 40 degrees above the horizon.

Toxic house plants poison more children than household chemicals.

Women blink twice as much as men.

Your eyes stay the same size your entire life, but your ears and nose never stop growing.

The first known contraceptive was crocodile dung, used by the ancient egyptians 3,000 years ago. It was very effective.

The filming of the movie Wayne's World took only two weeks.

If you were to spell out numbers, you would have to go all the way to the number 1,000 to use the first letter A.

Maine is the only state in the U. S with a one syllable name.

Research has found that millennials are the least religious generation in the history of the United States.

Peanut butter invented for people with no teeth so they could get protein in their diet.

There is a death metal band that has an African Grey parrot as its lead singer. They exist. **Check it out.**

PEOPLE

A group of research scientists went to subways in major cities around the world to test the air quality in the subways. The found that 15% of the particulates that people were breathing in the air comprised dead skin cells from other people. The majority from the head and feet, but some from other even more disgusting parts of the body.

Skin cell loss is always happening. The average person loses about 1 million skin cells per day. We lose about 8 pounds of dead skin cells per year. You never notice it happening, but it happens all the time.

Getting bitten by mosquitoes is nasty. There are things that draw them to some people more than others. People with type O blood get bitten almost twice as often as other blood types. People who exercise more are more likely to attract them because of lactic acid in their muscles. Drinking beer and being pregnant also increases your chances of being bitten.

One amazing survival story of a man survived both atomic bombs dropped on Japan in 1945. Tsutomu Yamaguchi was in Hiroshima on the morning of Aug 6. Tsutomu was in the bombing, but made his way home to Nagasaki before the second bomb dropped on his home city. He survived both bombings.

You will pass about 7,000 gallons of intestinal gas in your lifetime. That is equivalent to passing gas non stop for close to 9 days.

The average person will tell 2 lies per day that means you will tell almost 58,000 lies in your lifetime.

The average number of people you will know at any one time in your life is 290. The average number of people you will know over your lifetime is just under 2,000.

The city of Tokyo is the world's most populous city. Estimates put the population the Tokyo metropolitan area at 36.5 million.

The Chinese territory of Macau has the higher population density per area. They cram over 50,000 people per sq. mile into an area of 11.3 sq. miles.

The lowest population density in the world is the country of Mongolia. They have a population density of 5.1 people per sq. mile. Mongolia is the 18 largest country in the world.

The longest life expectancy is on the island of Monaco. The population is one of the wealthiest on earth, and they live an average of 89.7 years. They also have a very dense population of over 40,600 people per sq. mile. It is the most populated sovereign country in the world.

There are still 100 tribes in the Amazon rainforest that have never had contact with modern man.

The smallest independent republic in the world is the island of Nauru in the south Pacific. It has an area of 8.1 square miles and just over 9,000 inhabitants. They also hold the record for the most obese people in the world, with a body mass index average of over 35.

Your fingernails will grow in an average lifetime 6 feet 8 inches.

You will consume about 1,000 pounds of butter over your lifetime.

You will create 7,900 gallons of urine over your lifetime. You will spend about 22 days of your life peeing.

The average person has 1,000 trillion bacteria living on their skin and in their gut.

The Bubonic plague is the deadliest bacteria known to man. Over 25 million people died from it in the late 1800. The bacteria carried by rats and fleas and transmitted to humans from flea bites. There are antibiotics that treat it now, but no vaccines work well. There are about 650 cases reported each year, in Africa.

It is impossible to stop from insect parts getting into your food. In an average lifetime, you will eat about 115 pounds of insects.

The average person will eat close to 14,000 hen eggs in their lifetime. That's enough eggs to make an omelette the size of an Olympic size swimming pool.

The average person will eat 8.3 tons of potatoes in their lifetime. Potatoes are the fourth largest food crop in the world. Potato plants are poisonous so don't eat the plants.

There are 639 names muscles in the human body. The largest is the gluteus maximus, the muscle you sit on.

Your heart will beat around 3 trillion times in your life. It beats about 8 months before birth.

The nerve impulses in your body travel at around 430 miles per hour.

A sneeze can spew out particle at 100 miles per hour.

By the time you reach age 70, you will have shed over 100 pounds of skin.

The average woman will spend two years of her life working on her hair. The average man will spend about two weeks working on his hair.

The average person will blink 11,500 times per day. Each blink takes about .1 seconds. You will spend about 383 days of your life blinking 331 million times over your lifetime.

The average person will spend around $57,000 on clothes over their lifetime. Some people are much higher and much lower than the average.

There are 18.5 million people around the world that share your birthday.

There will be around 160 thousand people who will die on the same day you die.

You will lose about 296 gallons of blood over your lifetime.

You will sweat close to 560 gallons of sweat in your lifetime.

Over your lifetime you will speak about 439 million words. We all know someone who will more than double that.

You will laugh over 1.5 million times in your life.

You will use around 115 miles of toilet paper over your lifetime.

There are around 74,500 miles of blood vessels in the average human body.

There are around 7.6 billion people on the earth. We passed the 6 billion mark in 1999. We passed the 7 billion mark in late 2011. **Here is a link** to a world population site that is interesting.

On average you will drink over 12,000 gallons of water in your lifetime, and 1,500 gallons of milk.

The reason we know so little about the human brain is because there is about 200 billion neurons in the human brain. Each neuron has 7,000 synapses. Each synapses can make 1,000 connections. The human brain contains more connections than all the computers, routers and internet connections in the entire world.

The average person will spend close to one year of their life driving to and from work, around 330 days.

Ninety percent of all the people on the Earth live in the Northern hemisphere.

The population of California is higher than the population of all of Canada.

The average person will walk 125,000 miles in their lifetime.

The longest time for staying awake is not official any more. Guinness book of world record recognise 449 an hour as a record. That is 18 days. I can't imagine how bad is on your body to do that. In 1978 Guinness stopped using this record and stopped recognizing it because of the damage to the people trying to break it. When my wife was giving birth to my daughter, I was awake for almost 2 whole days. I felt terrible and would never even do that on purpose, I can't imagine 18 days. Don't try this.

PLANTS

World's tallest trees are the redwoods in northern California. One tree named Hyperion is 379 feet high. These trees are also long lived. This tree was a sapling about 2,000 years ago.

Bristlecone pines are the oldest living things on Earth. There are some that are five thousand years old. They grow at higher elevations, between 5,000 and 11,000 feet above sea level. I have seen several in person at Bryce Canyon National Park. The sign by the tree said it was over 2,000 years old.

The empress or foxglove tree can grow 15 feet or more in a year. They get used in parks and gardens. They have a fragrant orchid like bloom. It can be a pest and a problem of a tree in many places.

Foxglove bloom

Some species of bamboo can grow up to 35 inches in one day. And some can grow up to over 150 feet high.

Roses are close relatives to Apples, cherries, plums, raspberries, peaches, nectarines and almonds.

The corpse flower is one of the most unusual plants. It is very large and colorful. The bloom can grow up to 10 ft tall. The corpse flower is pollinated by bugs that eat rotting flesh, so it smells like rotting flesh when it is blooming. The bloom also warms up to 98 degrees to seem more like rotting flesh. This flower only blooms every 7 to 10 years. The bloom only lasts for 24 to 36 hours so it needs to get pollinated when it blooms.

Dandelions are weeds. They are a great source of vitamins A, C, iron, calcium and potassium. You can eat the leaves and the flowers.

Sunflowers move throughout the day tracking the sun.

Gas plants have nice greenery and nice flower similar to an orchid. On a calm still evening, you can light a match above the bloom and it will produce a small blue flame. It is said the seeds are flammable.

There are 630 different carnivorous plants around the world. Some live in soil, some are water plants. There are five ways carnivorous plants catch bugs.

- Some have slippery leaves that funnel toward the bottom of the plant. Bugs land on the leaves and slide into a pool of digestive enzymes.
- Flypaper traps. They have a sticky substance that the bugs land on and can't get away. The venus fly trap is one of these types of plants. Once the bug goes in, the trap closes and digests the bug.
- Snap traps. When a bug lands on the leaves the hairy spines on the leaves close around the bugs and they become food.
- Bladder traps. These are water plants. They suck the bugs and small animals out of the water like a vacuum, the bugs go into the bladder where they get digested.
- Lobster traps have tiny hairs all facing the same direction. This forces the bugs to walk toward the bottom of the plant leaves where there is a pool of digestive enzymes.

Photosynthesis is the process by which plants make food from the sunlight. They also need water to make their food.

Plants take in carbon dioxide and give off oxygen. This makes it possible for us to live on Earth.

The carbon dioxide, water and sun combine to create glucose. Glucose gives the plant energy that helps it grow and produce more leaves.

There are over 80,000 species of edible plants on earth, yet 90% of our food from plants comes from only 30 of them.

There are 70,000 plant species with medicinal properties.

Only one percent of the plants in the rainforest have been tested for medicinal use.

Caffeine evolved as a natural insecticide. It will paralyze the insects that eat the plant the chemical is on.

Hops and marijuana are from the same plant family.

Native Americans planted beans, squash and corn together so they could use and help each other. The corn gave a place for the beans to climb while providing nitrogen for the soil and the squash covered the ground to keep down the weeds.

The trees that Johnny Appleseed planted were not to feed people. The tart apples he planted were more for making alcohol.

The word Pineapple comes from European explorers who thought the fruit looked like a pine cone with flesh like an apple.

From a botanical point of view, Tomatoes, avocados and pumpkins are fruit because the fruit carries the seeds.

The average strawberry has 200 seeds. It is the only fruit that bears its seeds on the outside of the fruit.

Peanuts are not nuts. They are a member of the bean family.

There are over 200,000 identified plant species, and the list gets bigger every day.

SCIENCE

Absolute zero is the coldest temperature that exists. That temperature is -460 degrees Fahrenheit, minus 269 degrees Centigrade, or 0 degrees Kelvin.

When helium gas is at a temperature close to absolute zero, it will turn to a liquid that will do things that are unusual. If in an open container, it will flow up the side of the container and over the top.

An individual blood cell will travel full circuit of the human body in one minute.

41 new species of plants discovered by scientists every day.

This is not science. It is more like anti science. There is a group of people called the flat earth society that say they believe the earth is flat. Their name is the flat earth society and covenant people's church. They say the earth is a flat disc. They say the Bible says the earth is flat. There is no Hebrew word for sphere so they say Bible reference that interpret the earth is spherical are saying it is a disc. The flat earth Facebook group claims to have 378,000 members as of this year.

If you drop a ball from a high place and spin it, it will fly. It's called the Magnus effect. **Check out the video.**

If you drop a bowling ball and a feather from the same height, the bowling ball will hit the ground first. If you do this in a large vacuum chamber, they will fall at the same speed and hit the ground at the same time. **Check the video.**

Traveling at the speed of light it would take you 13 seconds to travel around the earth.

The strongest living creature on earth is the gonorrhea bacteria. They can move 100,000 times their weight.

There are more living organisms on your skin than there are humans alive on the earth.

The average human male will produce about 86 million sperm per day.

The earth spins at 1,000 mph. It travels through space at 67,000 miles per hour.

There are over one million earthquakes on earth every year.

It would take over an hour for a heavy object to drop to the bottom of the deepest part of the ocean.

Plutonium was the first man made element. Glenn Seaborg and his colleagues at the university of chicago in 1942 were the first to weight the new element.

Sound travels 15 times faster through steel than it does through air.

The celsius scale makes more sense than the Fahrenheit scale. 0 degrees celsius is freezing and 100 degrees is the boiling point of water. The most logical way to tell temperature would be to use the Kelvin scale, but it would be difficult for many people. The temperature of freezing Kelvin is 273.16 degrees and the boiling point of water is 100 degrees higher at 373.16 degrees. 0 degrees Kelvin is absolute zero.

The tilt of the earth affects the temperature being lower in the winter in the northern hemisphere, not the distance from the sun. The earth is several million miles closer to the sun in the winter than it is in the summer.

Infrared motions detectors will not work if the surrounding walls and floors are higher than the normal human temperature of 98.6 degrees.

Earth is the only planet not named after a Greek God.

SPACE

The tallest known mountain is not on Earth. The tallest mountain known to man is Olympus mons on Mars. The mountain is over 15 miles high. Over 3 times the height of Mt. Everest.

The largest planet in our solar system is Jupiter. It is 317 times the size of earth. The planet has 63 moons. Jupiter is a mini solar system. It has the shortest day of any planet in our solar system of 9 hours 55 minutes. It has a mean temperature of -234 F. It orbits the sun once every 11.8 earth years. The red spot on Jupiter is a storm that has gone on for at least 350 years. The storm travels counterclockwise and takes about 6 earth days to go around the planet. It is so big 3 earths could fit into the storm. Jupiter's moon Ganymede is larger than the planet Mercury.

The cost for the average taxpayer in the United States for supporting the international space station is around $12.23.

The worst disasters in manned space flight has happened twice. The first on launch and the second on reentry. Close to 300 manned space flights have occurred. The space shuttle Challenger exploded in Feb. 2011, 73 seconds after liftoff in Florida. 7 astronauts died in the disaster. The second with 7 fatalities was when the space shuttle Columbia disintegrated on reentry because of an incident during launch where a fuel tank hit the wing and damaged the tiles to protect the shuttle on reentry.

The first humans to set foot on the moon were American astronauts, Neil Armstrong, and Buzz

Aldrin. July 21, 1969. The landed the eagle lunar module in the sea of tranquillity.

The first human to go into space was Russian cosmonaut Yuri Gagarin in 1961.

If you went out into space, you would explode before you suffocated because of the lack of air pressure.

SPORTS

NFL

The top scoring player ever in the NFL as of this writing is Morten Andersen. He is only about 80 points ahead of Adam Vinatieri who is still playing. Anderson scored 2,544 points. Anderson also holds the record for most games by a player, 382.

Gary Anderson hold the record for most points in a season with 164 in 1998 with the Minnesota Vikings. 59 pat's and 39 fg.

The top scoring non kicker is Jerry Rice. Rice scored 1,256 points in his career. There is no one playing that is anywhere close to Rice for scoring.

The Denver Broncos scored 606 points to be the highest scoring team for a season in the NFL in 2013. They were 13 - 3 that year and lost to Seattle in the super bowl.

The Green Bay Packers hold the record for scoring the fewest points in a season with 419 points in 2008. They were 6 - 10 that year.

This is the most amazing record in the NFL, and will last forever. Ernie Nevers on Nov, 28 1929 scored 40 points in one game. That is not even the most amazing part. He scored 6 touchdowns and kicked 4 extra points to account for all the points for his team in a 40 - 6 victory. He was fullback for the Chicago Cardinals and they routed the Chicago Bears.

Devin Hester set an amazing record of 20 kick returns for touchdowns in his career.

Ben Roethlisberger set an amazing record just this week in the game with the Raven on Dec. 10 2017. He passed for 506 yards. There have been 21 games in NFL history where the quarterback threw for over 500 yards. Ben has done it 3 of those times. No other quarterback has done it more than once, and only 18 others have ever done it.

George Bland played in the NFL for 26 years. He was a quarterback and a placekicker. He retired at age 48. He also leads the league with most kick attempts in a career at 959. He also holds the record for the most field goals missed at 304.

Jason Hanson, kicker for the Detroit Lions played his entire 21 year career with the same team. The longest player playing with the same team. He played in 327 games.

Stephen Gostkowski made 523 consecutive kicks without a miss. This record will also last forever.

Jeff Feagles played in the most consecutive games. He was a punter who played in 352 consecutive games.

The most consecutive games played with the same team was Jim Marshall at 270. The amazing thing about this record is Marshal was a defensive end. He was part of the Purple People eaters of the Minnesota Vikings in the 1970s.

Jim Marshall is also famous for the wrong way run. He picked up a fumble and ran 88 yard into the wrong end zone scoring a safety for the other team.

Jerry Rice scored 208 touchdowns in his career. Emmitt Smith is second with 175. Rice's record likely will last forever.

Jerry Rice also holds the record for most receiving yards, 22,895. There are 4 other players between 15 and 16,000 yards. That is almost three and a half miles behind Rice.

Brett Favre holds the record for most consecutive games started by a QB at 297.

TRACK AND FIELD

Roger Bannister was the first man to break the 4 minute mile May 6, 1954.

Hicham El Guerrouj of Morocco holds the record for the mile. In 1999 he set the record of 3:43.13 in Rome Italy.

The longest running race was the 1929 transcontinental footrace from New York to LA. The course was 3,635 miles. Won by Johnny Salo from Finland with a time of 525 hours, 57 minutes and 20 seconds. The race was an unbelievable feat. He only won by 2 minutes and 43 seconds.

The fastest 100m. Considered the fastest runner. Jamaica's Usain Bolt set the record in 2009 at 9.58

sec. Florence Griffith Joyner set the women's record of 10.49 sec. In 1988.

The record for men's high jump is one of the longest standing records in track and field. Javier Sotomayor from Cuba set the record with a jump of 8 ft ¼ in in 1993.

GOLF

Tiger Woods was the youngest player to win the Masters. Tiger won the 1997 Masters on April 13th at 21 years 104 days old.

There are over 125,000 golf balls hit in the water on hole 17, the island green at the stadium course at Sawgrass every year.

The lowest score in a single round in a PGA tour event is 58. Jim Furyk did it Aug 7 2016. Six time there have been rounds of 59. Furyk also has one of those. He is also the only golfer to have 2 sub 60 shot rounds.

Phil Mickelson is the most well known left handed golfer. The strange thing is he is right handed. His father was a lefty and Phil learned to play with his father, He learned left handed and never changed. I am the opposite. I am left handed but golf right handed.

The first golf tournament televised across the country was the 1953 world championship of golf. Lew Worsham holed out for an eagle on the final hole to win by one shot.

There have been 4 verified hole in ones on a par 5. The longest was at a high altitude course in Colorado. July 4, 2002 Mike Crean teed off on the 517 yard 9th hole at Green Valley Ranch course outside Denver. Because of the distance, no one saw the ball go in the hole. When they got to the green, the ball was in the hole. He and his playing partners signed affidavits confirming the hole in one. This shot known as a Condor.

In 2010 Richard Lewis played an unbelievable 611 rounds of golf in one calendar year. He played everyone on the same course, the Four Seasons resort in Irving Texas.

During world war II, 1943, 44 and 1945, they canceled the Masters and Augusta National closed, and the course used to raise cattle and turkeys to support the war effort.

The longest put in a tournament made by Bob Cook during the 1976 four ball tournament on the 18th hole at St. Andrews. He sunk a put of 140 feet 2 and ¾ inches.

Sam Sneed holds the record for the most tour wins in history at 82. Tiger woods is 3 behind. Tiger is still playing, He still has a change to take the lead.

Jack Nicklaus holds the record for the most major wins at 18. Tiger is also second in this category. This is the record that Tiger has always wanted to beat. Tiger has 14 major wins. It seems unlikely that Tiger can pass Jack on majors, but Jack won his 6th masters at age 46. Tiger was 42 years old on Dec 30, 2017. He could still win more.

There are 320 to 432 dimples on a regulation golf ball. The number of dimples affect the ball flight. The optimum numbers is around the 336 spot.

Before the 1920s, there were no tees. Golfers built their own tees from a pile of sand on the tee box.

Tiger woods shot his first hole in one at 6 years old. He has had 17 more since then.

The oldest golf course is not St. Andrews as many people think. The oldest existing course is Musselburgh links in Scotland. For the record, the course opened in 1672, but may have been there since the late 1560s.

There are 4 majors called the grand slam if you win them all. The Masters, The British Open, The United States Open, and the PGA Championship. No one has ever won all 4 in the same year. Tiger won all 4 in a row, but not in the same year.

The longest golf course in the world is the International in Massachusetts. The course is a par 77 and is 8325 yards long.

The longest hole in the world is is the par 7, seventh hole at the Satsuki golf club in Japan, at 962 yards.

The highest golf course in the world. There are several that claim the highest. All are over 12,000 feet. You can get altitude sickness from playing any of these courses without getting acclimated before playing. The reason for the dispute is how they measure the elevation. Do you go from the highest point, the highest average, or the highest low point. There was a course in Peru that closed in 1993 that was over 14,000 feet at its lowest point. You needed oxygen to play this course.

The highest in North America is Copper creek golf club on Copper mountain in Colorado. The highest tee box is at 9,863 feet above sea level. The course is open only a few months of the year because of the snow.

Scotland has the highest number of golf courses per capita in the world. There are about 35,000 golf courses in the world, 45% are in the United States.

Golf balls fly farther on hotter days. The denseness of the air and the balls construction makes hot days better for longer shots.

Tiger was the youngest ever to win the Masters at age 21. Jack was the youngest before that at age 23.

Jack had the record for the youngest and oldest to win the masters when he won it in 1986 at age 46. He had that record till 1997 when Tiger won the masters at 21.

Golf is the only professional sport that having the lowest score is the best.

Golf is a good exercise. If you walk and carry your clubs you can burn around 1700 calories in a round of golf. Few players do this though. If you ride a cart and the cart carries your clubs, it is much less. Still better than sitting at a desk.

80% of golfers will never have a handicap less than 18. If you do, you are in a group of elite golfers.

For the average golfer, the odds of a hole in one are 12,500 to 1. I have never had one. My closest was about 1 inch away on a par 3 107 yard hole. Going by those numbers, you should have one in your first 700 rounds of golf. If you play 18 holes, you have 18 chances per round at a hole in one. Still waiting for mine.

The first golf balls made of leather stuffed with feathers. After that the construction went to wood. New golf balls are constructed of rubber and plastic compounds. There are differences, but most have a rubber core. Some have a liquid center. The outer white part is plastic and rubber combination, or blends of plastic. The materials affect the flight, control, amount of spin and durability.

Because the first balls were hand made and took a lot of time. The Cost of the balls were around $14 each. Far too expensive for any non royalty to purchase. Golf was a rich person's game

BASEBALL

The longest nine inning baseball game was the second game of a doubleheader between the Yankees and Red Sox on August 18, 2006. The game lasted 4 hr. 45 min.. The game was at Fenway Park in Boston and the Yankees won 14-11.

The longest major league baseball game by innings was the White sox against the Brewers in 1984. The White sox won 7-6 in 25 innings. The time of this game was 8 hr and 6 minutes. There was one game longer by innings. In 1920 the Brooklyn Robins and the Boston Braves played to a 1-1 tie. The game ended because of darkness.

The first world series was between Pittsburgh and boston in 1903. It was a best of 9 games. Boston won 5 games to 3.

The New York Yankees have won the world series 27 times and had 40 appearances in the world series. It is a money thing, but not aways.

Cal Ripken Jr. did not miss a game in 16 seasons. He played in 2,632 consecutive games from 1982 to 1998.

Pete Rose hold two amazing records. Most games played and most hits. He played in 3,562 games and had 4,256 hits.

Barry Bonds holds the record for the most home runs in a season at 73.

Barry Bonds also has the record for a career at 762.

Take me out to the ballgame, written by Jack Norworth and Albert Von Tilzer in 1908. Neither of the men had ever been to a baseball game.

No woman has ever played in a major league baseball game.

The lifespan of a major league baseball is 5 to 7 pitches.

Baseball started in the U.S. Baseball now played in over 100 countries around the world.

Mickey Mantle holds the top two spots for the longest home runs in baseball history. 565 feet and 643 feet. The 643 foot shot was an estimate because the ball went over the roof and out of the ballpark.

Hot dogs are the most popular ballpark food. Baseball fans eat over 21 million hot dogs per year at baseball games.

Ray Chapman playing for the Cleveland Indians on August 16, 1920 is the only player ever killed by a pitch. The pitch hit him in the head and died from the hit in the hospital the next day.

The first radio broadcast of a baseball game was by KDKA in Pittsburgh on Aug 5 1921. The Pirates beat the Phillies 8-5. It was also the first live play-by-play of a baseball game.

The first televised game was on Aug 26 1939. The Cincinnati reds against the Brooklyn Dodgers.

Major league baseballs must have lacing with 108 stitches. It must be 9.00 to 9.25 inches around and between 5.0 and 5.25 ounces, and made of 2 pieces of cowhide laced together with red waxed cotton stitches.

Philadelphia Phillies star Richie Ashburn fouled off two consecutive pitches. The first one hit and broke the nose of a woman in the stands. As she was being treated, the second foul ball hit her again.

The Atlanta Braves started their team in Boston as the Boston Beaneaters.

 Jackie Robinson broke the color barrier in 1947 and became the first black player in Major league baseball. He faced racism everyday. This was 8 years before the civil rights movement started. He was a key to the Brooklyn Dodgers winning the world championship in 1955, and he had a hall of fame career in the major leagues.

The Red Sox sold Babe Ruth to the Yankees for $125,000 dollars cash in 1920. He was just coming into the peak of his career. The reason they sold him was, Ruth wanted a pay raise to $20,000 per year and the Red Sox owners would not pay him.

Hank Aaron broke Ruths home run record of 714 in 1974. This was one of those unbreakable records.

The first all star game played in 1933. 20 of the 36 players in the game went on to the hall of fame. The AL won 4-2.

Roberto Clemente was a great star for the Pittsburgh Pirates. He was also a great humanitarian. He was always helping people. He was on a flight taking supplies to Puerto Rico when the plane crashed and he died.

Pete Rose was one of the best love player and best players ever. Rose caught betting on baseball games in 1989. There was never proof he bet on his team. But he received a lifetime ban from baseball. It kept him out of the hall of fame.

George Steinbrenner buys the Yankees in 1973. He paid $10 million for the team, that is now worth over 2 billion dollars

Major league baseball pitcher Gaylord Perry said in 1963, "they will put a man on the moon before I hit a home run." On July 20, 1969, one hour after Neil Armstrong put his foot on the moon, Perry hit the first and only home run of his career.

NBA

Basketball invented by a gym teacher in 1891 to give the kids something to do on rainy days.

The game started being played on a court with chicken wire fence around the court to keep the ball on the court. There were a lot of injuries from the fence.

There were two teams of 9 players each. There was also no dribbling in the early game. Moving the ball was by passing only.

The first baskets were peach baskets with the bottoms in them. The ball had to taken from the basket each time.

The baskets nailed to the balcony. Spectators in the balcony would interfere with the shots until backboards stopped that.

The first balls used were soccer balls. They were slippery and didn't work well.

Early in basketball, there was a jump ball after every basket. I can see why they changed that rule.

In 1946 the early NBA had a team in Providence RI, called the steamrollers. The were there for 3 seasons and had a record of 46-122.

Kobe's middle name is Bean. Kobe was not a top ten pick. Picked number 13 in the draft.

Before playing in the NBA, Wilt Chamberlain was with the Harlem Globetrotters. He spent only one year with the team, 1999 to 2000 season. His number is retired as a globetrotter.

The three point shot started in the ABA and wasn't part of the NBA until the 1979-1980 season.

Moses Malone was the first NBA star to not go to college. He spent 19 years in the NBA. He went to 12 consecutive all star games. Malone, inducted in 2001 into the hall of fame.

LeBron James also never went to college.

Kobe Bryant also did not go to college. He was the youngest player to start in the NBA at 18 ½ years old.

Wilt Chamberlain had 55 rebounds in one game. He also scored 100 points in a single game. Wilt had 32 games in his career with over 60 points scored.

The Boston Celtics have won more championships than any other NBA team, 17. The Lakers are second with 16. The next closest team is the Bulls with 6.

Carl Lewis drafted by the Bills in 1984 a month before he won 4 golds at the olympics. Although he never played organized basketball. Lewis drafted as well by the Dallas Cowboys even though he never played football.

Kareem Abdul Jabbar made only 1 three point shot in his career.

Michael Jordan's contract with Nike paid him more money per year than all the Nike factory workers in Malaysia made each year combined.

NHL

The ice on a hockey rink is ¾ of an inch thick. The ice temperature is 16 degrees.

The lines on the ice are in the ice. They are on the ice at ½ inch thick, then the rest of the ice goes over the top of it.

Before 1914 hockey pucks got laid on the ice. Because of all the injuries to the referees they changed the rules so they could drop the puck.

In 1971 Bobby Orr signed the first million dollar deal in hockey. He signed a 5 year deal for $200,000 per year.

Wayne Gretzky scored 378 goals in his final year in pee wee hockey. This is one of those records that will last forever.

Gretzky turned pro at age 17. He played for one month for the Indianapolis racers before being traded to the Edmonton Oilers.

Gretzky has 2857 career points in the NHL. That is 970 points ahead of Second place. Another record that will never change. The most amazing part of this is that if you took off the 894 goals he scored, he would still be the leading scorer in NHL history with just his assists.

Gretzky scored 50 goals in 39 games. The only player to score 50 goals in less than 50 games.

Gretzky is the only player to score 200 points in a season. He did it four times.

Gretzky scored 92 goals in one season. Only 4 other players have scored over 65 in a season, The next closes was Brett Hull with 86. Mario Lemieux with 85, and two other players have scored 70.

Gretzky holds or shares 60 all time NHL records.

This is one of the strangest thing to happen in a hockey game. In 1930 in a game, goalie Abie Goldberry caught on fire when a puck hit a pack of matches he had in his pocket. Goldberry was severely burned before his teammates put the fire out.

The Slovakian women's hockey team qualified for the 2010 olympics by beating the Bulgarian team 82-0.

There are Over 24 errors in the engraving on the stanley cup.

In 1919 there was no winner in the championship of the Stanley cup finals. The series called after 6 games. The final game canceled because almost all the players and the coach of the Montreal Canadian were in the hospital with flu.

Because there is one cup used each year, repairs to the cup have been needed several times. The cup has been tossed into a bonfire and has fallen into an icy canal over the years.

TENNIS

They use around 52,000 tennis balls for the Wimbledon tournament.

Wimbledon is the oldest tennis tournament in the world. Played at the All England Club in Wimbledon. The first one was in 1877.

The Wimbledon tournament uses around 55,000 balls during the event.

During ww2, several bombs hit center court at Wimbledon. It took 9 years to rebuild the center court.

TECHNOLOGY

In 1913, Henry Ford created the original moving assembly line. He wished to build his cars in Highland Park Michigan, close to Detroit. They cut the time to make a car from 12.5 hours per vehicle to 1 hour and 33 minutes. This revolutionised the manufacturing industry.

The firefox logo is not a fox. The logo animal is a red panda. The red panda is native to southern China.

Cd players read the disc from the inside moving out as it reads. This is the opposite or records. Most people think compact discs read the same, not true.

The term qwerty keyboard is from the first 6 keys on the top letter line of the standard keyboard.

One state in the United States has all the letters in the name on the same line of the keyboard, Alaska.

The Dvorak keyboard is a simplified version of the keyboard. They say it will help people type faster, and with fewer mistakes. Not everyone agrees. Most people would have trouble switching. Here is what it looks like.

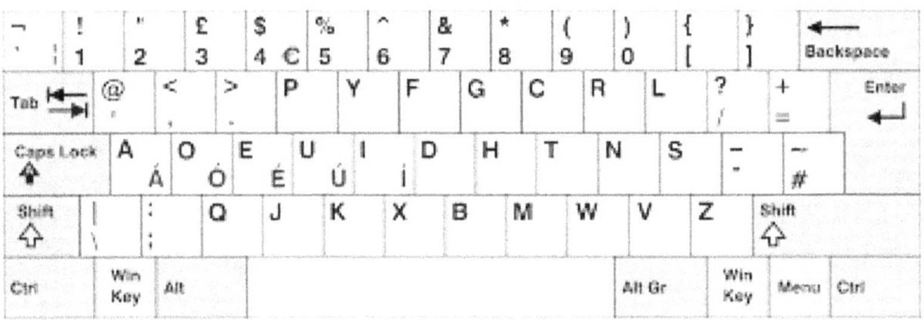

Wikimedia Commons

Apples Macintosh name inspired by the MacIntosh apple.

Phantom vibration syndrome is the medical name when you feel your phone vibrating and it isn't.

A ¼ inch square of silicone can contain the computing ability of the first computer. The original 1949 computer covered a city block.

UNIVERSE

This is the hardest category to cover. Most of what there is about the universe is a theory. Many of the theories based on things we have to assume are there to even make the theories. Many of them are interesting to read about, but we don't know or understand them. These things are things we know.

The Andromeda galaxy is the largest galaxy in our group of galaxies. It contains about 1 trillion stars. It is far bigger than the milky way galaxy. This is of one of the ones we know about.

Black holes are one of the most interesting things in space. They are what happens to a star when it dies and collapses into itself. The gravity of a black hole is so strong, even light can't escape the gravitational pull. Black holes can be small or large. The small ones will not form by collapsing stars. Science is not sure how small ones formed. Scientist have found proof that large galaxies have a supermassive black hole at the center of the galaxy. The one at the center of the Milky way, called Sagittarius and has a mass of 4 million of our suns. Our sun is much too small to become a black hole.

The nearest red supergiant star to earth. Betelgeuse in the constellation Orion. It is about 427 light years from our solar system. It is about 500 times the size of our sun.

The universe is huge, maybe never ending. The size is amazing. As an example, the earth has a diameter at the equator of just under 8,000 miles. The Milky way galaxy, which is a small galaxy in a vast universe has a diameter of around 621 quadrillion miles.

Our sun is one of at least 100 billion stars in the Milky way galaxy. Scientists estimate there are over 100 billion galaxies in the observable universe.

If you could travel at the speed of light. It would take 100,000 years to travel across our tiny Milky Way galaxy.

Venus is the slowest rotating planet in our solar system. It takes 243 earth days for Venus to rotate once on its axis. It takes 225 earth days for the planet to rotate once around the sun. Therefore a day is longer than a year on Venus when measured in earth days.

Neutron stars are the fast rotating objects in the universe. Because of the pulses of light given off, we can measure the rate of the pulse and calculate the rotation. Some of them are rotating at one quarter the speed of light.

One spoonful of matter from a neutron star would weigh around one billion tons.

In March 2013 Voyager 1 became the first manmade object to leave our solar system.

Most of the universe is silent. With no medium to travel through, there is no sound. Space is dead silent.

WEATHER

Tornadoes are very dangerous weather phenomena. The United States gets a lot of tornadoes every year, but the Netherlands has more per land area than any place in the world.

There are about 40 lightning strikes every second on the earth. Each lightning bolt can have up to 100,000 volts of electricity.

The worst hailstorm ever happened in Bangladesh on April 14, 1986. They had a storm that contained hailstones up to 2 pounds and killed 92 people.

Cherrapunji Meghalaya India has the unbelievable record of the most rain in a month and the most rain in 12 months. In July 1861 they received 366 inches of rain. The 12 months from August 1860 thru July 1861 they received an unbelievable 1,041.75 inches of rain. 30 feet of rain in a month, and 86 feet of rain in that year.

Cilaos Reunion in the Indian ocean got 73 inches of rain in 24 hours from March 15 into March 16, 1952.

Browning Montana experienced the greatest temperature change in one day. The temp dropped from 44F to -56F. A 100 degree change in temperature.

Before 1950 Hurricane names were random. For the next 3 years they named them by alphabet with a list that didn't change. That caused problems because they had the same name storms every year. Then they named them after human female names. Next changed to alternate male and female names. Any storms that are terrible and cause a major loss of life or extensive damage will have its name retired and not used again. Since 1954 there have been around 80 names retired, depending on the names retired in this year.

Yuma Arizona is the sunniest place on earth. They have 4,000 hours of sunshine per year.

The coldest temp ever recorded on earth was at Vostok station Antarctica in 1983.. -129.8 Fahrenheit

The strongest wind ever recorded was on Mt Washington, New Hampshire, USA at an amazing 231 mph.

There are around 2000 thunderstorms going on around the earth at any one time.

There are 100,000 thunderstorms in the United States every year.

There are 16,000,000 thunderstorms around the world every year.

Mt. Rainier Washington received 90 feet of snow in the winter of 1972.

The warmest temperature ever recorded in Antarctica was in 1974. 59 degrees.

Former chief justice of the supreme court was a weatherman in the army before going to Stanford and getting his law degree.

You can tell the temperature by counting the chirps of a cricket. Count the chirps in 15 seconds and add 37 to get the temperature in Fahrenheit.

Prospect creek Alaska holds the record for the coldest temperature in the United States at minus 80 degrees.

One inch of rain falling over one acre of land is 27,000 gallons of water.

Hilo Hawaii is the wettest city in the U.S. They receive 128 inches of rain per year.

In 1934 the Mt. Washington observatory in New Hampshire recorded the fastest wind speed recorded on earth at 231 mph.

Texas gets the most tornadoes every year in the world at 2110.

The largest tornado recorded was in Nebraska. It was over 2 ½ miles wide.

The worst hurricane in the U.S. hit Galveston Texas in 1900. 8,000 people died in this storm.

The fastest winds on earth are in a tornado. Wind speeds up to 318 mph can happen in tornados.

January 10, 1911 in Rapid City S.D. the temperature dropped from 55 degrees to 8 degrees in 15 minutes.

Aomori City in northern Japan receives on average 26 feet of snow per year. The snowiest major city in the world.

Around one billion tons of rain falls on the earth every minute of every day.

La Paz Bolivia has an average annual temperature of 50 degrees Fahrenheit, but has never recorded a temperature of zero or below.

CONCLUSION

There are millions of fun facts, about everything you can think of. The facts are fun to read, and you can really learn a lot about a lot of things. When you read through these things you will think, how did I never read that before?

If you have any suggestions you would like see in the book, or if you have any comments, email me at steve@stevepease.net and I will get back to you.

Reviews of books on Amazon make a big difference in getting seen on the website. If you thought the book was a fun read and good information, Please go to the review page and leave a review.

Thank again for reading, and check out my other books at stevepease.net.

ABOUT ME

My name is Steve Pease. I live in the Northern suburbs of the Twin Cities in Minnesota.

I have been writing for about six years. I've written several hundred articles for HubPages and for examiner over the years. For Examiner I wrote a column for the Twin Cities on Disc golf, and one on Cycling in the Twin Cities, and one on Exercise and fitness for the Twin cities.

I write on subjects I am passionate about, disc golf, exercise, photography, cycling, fishing, and topics that deal with Christian beliefs.

My father is a retired minister, and he has written many books. I have edited many of them and have them available on my site that cover many topics of interest to Christians today. I have also written an Old Testament trivia book on my own.

 I have been playing disc golf since 1978 and love the sport. The greatest thing about disc golf is at age fifty eight I'm still very competitive and beat players much younger than me. Disc golf is a sport you can play at almost any age as long as you can walk.

I have taken several hundred thousand pictures over the last 35 years and I'm always trying to improve my photography. My goal is always to take the big shots I can. I want people to say wow when they look at my shots. I went through the photography course at New York Institute of photography many years ago. What I learned from the course and my years of experience was worth every dollar.

The key to be a great photographer is to see things that most people don't see, or in a way they didn't see it. My favorite types of photography are landscape, portrait, animals and infrared. I have shot several weddings and spend hundreds of hours just exploring different places looking for great things to take pictures of.

I have been an avid fisherman since I was a kid. I have had 2 bass fishing boats over the years, but I enjoy fishing for my kayak. I have a sit inside old town kayak, and a sit on top feelfree Moken 12 fishing kayak. I also have two old town canoes for going to

the boundary waters wilderness area or just paddling
around lakes in my area.

  The hardest part about fishing from a kayak is trying
to decide what not to take with me. As with most bass
fishermen I have tons of equipment, and I always feel
I need to take it all with me, just in case. Kayak fishing
has made me downsize just to make everything fit in
my kayak.

I spend most of my fishing time catching bass and
northern pike. But if I'm looking for a good meal, you
can beat crappies and sunfish. I have spent most of
my time fishing freshwater, but I have caught
saltwater fish. The biggest was a 380 pound bull
shark off Key West Florida in 1985.

I have also have loved biking and exercising since I
was in my early teens. I like to read nonfiction book so
I can keep learning new things all the time. Many of
the things I learn I want to share with you and help
enrich your life. I want to pass on the knowledge I
have learned over the years and share it with others.

Thanks again

Check out my book site for other good books.
Stevepease. net